NO RELATION

NO RELATION

PAULA CARTER

Black
Lawrence
Press

Black Lawrence Press

www.blacklawrence.com

Executive Editor: Diane Goettel
Book and Cover Design: Amy Freels
Cover Art: "An Inkling" by Justin Santora

Copyright © Paula Carter 2017
ISBN: 978-1-62557-981-2

Published 2017 by Black Lawrence Press.
Printed in the United States.

Some names and identifying details have been changed to protect the privacy of individuals.

For my mother

ACT I

ALMOST MOTHER

When James calls me, to tell me he has again married, I am already a new woman. I'm living in a new city, with a new job, and new friends, most of whom don't know him or understand that I was almost a mother. I wear zippy clothes—money in my pocket—and frequent all the coffee shops in my neighborhood—time on my hands. But a few days later, when it is his youngest son's 10th birthday, I wonder again how it is I am that new woman.

Where is the other one? She is still here. Sometimes I see her, peeking out, watching me laugh with my new friends. She hovers over my bent head and brushes back the hair from my temple—unsure who else to care for.

Like a ghost that can't cross over she stands beside me in line at the grocery store when I buy Lean Cuisine and blueberries and yogurt. She stands beside me while this girl at the gym explains how her son is wetting the bed. We hold our tongue thinking of the time James and I bought that used washer and dryer because of his oldest son and how we then had to move it from house to house.

COUP DE FOUDRE

This is before. It is the summer after my first year of graduate school. I am a student assistant at the Lilly Library, where in the stacks— accessible to staff only—live the letters of Sylvia Plath and the first English edition of *Pinocchio*. My job is to sit in the reading room and keep watch, make sure none of the scholars, who travel here from Philadelphia and U.C. Davis, bend down the corner of a gilded page, pocket a miniature book the size of my thumbnail. Mostly I stare out the windows, past the long green curtains like something from the *The Sound of Music*.

Outside, the hopeful spring leaves of southern Indiana are playing in a warm wind and the smell of sycamore moves through campus. I keep notes with a pencil—pens are not allowed in the reading room—of words that strike me as good sounding in succession. Pink king yellow hat. Tiny icky yucky black.

I am 26. In the slanting sunlight I see dust hovering in the air. Perhaps it is from the manuscripts that once sat on the desk of Gordon Lish. I am breathing gold. The world is perched atop my index finger, when into the room walks a man whose sleeves are rolled up and hair is pulled into a ponytail. He is wearing black leather shoes and is skinny like a beanpole. A smile passes between us. We will discuss that smile for years to come. It will become a part of our mythology. I ask him what he is studying and learn he is a young photography professor. His name is James.

A friend will say to me, "Sometimes it is like your heart recognizes someone you are going to spend a lot of time with before you've spent any of that time."

It is weeks before I find out he has children.

NO

James told me he had kids, over the phone, after our first date and I cried. He wanted me to meet them right away. But I said no, I wasn't ready. I wanted to hold onto my fantasy a little longer—the fantasy of young love. They say resistance to what is is the root of all unhappiness. Well, I guess here is where the seed begins to germinate.

OTHER PEOPLE'S KIDS

At the Dairy Queen there are a bunch of kids hanging around. A couple families and a softball team. I have walked over here alone as a treat to myself. Summer is just dawning.

The kids are all doing different things. These two are chasing each other around a table and this one has his face buried in his cone so when he pulls up, his nose is white and dripping—ice cream and snot mixed together. A little girl with blond curly hair is crying and her mother is talking to someone else. The mother's hand is held out towards the little girl, but the little girl doesn't see it and the mother is busy in her conversation.

They are loud. So loud. And I think, "I can't do this."

THE FIRST TIME

The first time I met Caleb and Alex, they hid under their beds.

"I'm not sure what happened to the boys," their father said, winking as I entered the small house. Each room was painted a bright color: yellow, terracotta red, mint green. After his divorce from the boys' mother, James had needed some cheer. He looked at me expectantly.

"Where could they be?" I asked. I knew nothing about kids.
"I don't know?" James pointed to their shared bedroom.

I knew it was my cue to go in and discover them, but I hesitated. I was nervous about the meeting and wished they had just been standing by the door, with their little hands outstretched to shake mine. But here we were playing hide and seek right off the bat.

I inched towards their door and once I stepped inside that was all it took. They burst forth, giggling. Two small boys with sandy brown hair. They jumped up and down, not getting close enough to touch me, but hovering in my radius. Immediately I was overcome by the smell: milk and cotton and sleep and dirty feet. As a teenager, I babysat for a family with two boys and here was the smell—the exact same smell—that had hung in their bedroom. Little boy potpourri. It was comforting. It reminded me that at one time, at 16, I had felt that I could handle two little boys without a hitch. I was Red Cross Babysitter Certified.

"What's your favorite color?" Caleb asked.

"Green." That was his too.

"What's your favorite food?" he asked.

"Quiche," I said.

The bounding stopped for a moment. Caleb looked at me skeptically. Then said, "Mine's pizza."

Alex was more reluctant, but eventually he began offering me toys to inspect and approve. He carried over a Transformer and set it in my hands then turned to find something else. This was going well, I thought.

That night was the Fourth of July, so we piled into James's station wagon and headed to the park to watch the fireworks. We found a spot to lay our blanket and began to wait. But, we had miscalculated the evening's events, arriving an hour after the boy's bedtime and more than an hour before the fireworks began without water or snacks. Soon the boys appeared to be dying of thirst, Caleb coughing, asking a nearby stranger for water.

By the time we left, without seeing a single firework, Alex had dumped my purse out onto the grass and was calling me "poopy Paula."

LOVE SONG

We are going to see the bats. We are three, James, his youngest son, and me. The bats will appear at dusk, swooping low among the trees at Bryan Park. They are easy to miss, because at first they look like swallows. But, if you look closely, you'll see that they move differently—less of a glide and more of a dance. I say this to Alex as we walk, thinking he will find it interesting. Alex is looking down into the grass, scouting, and he tells me that his class went on a field trip to a cave filled with thousands and thousands of bats and so he already knows. I look to James and he shakes his head no. Alex is wearing a sleeveless tank top that shows his plump, 4-year-old arms and I am tempted to squeeze them, but it is safer to take James's hand in my own. James leans over and kisses my head. Ahead of us, Alex spies something and calls out, "Dad!" staccato, breathless. James goes to him and squats down and the two of them look at a family of mushrooms growing under a fledgling tree.

When we get to the bench in the middle of the park, James lies down to look at the sky but Alex is restless. He asks me if I'll play tag.

I make a sudden move and he takes off running. His motor skills are still developing and his legs kick out on either side as he runs. I feel silly careening after him, unsure of what I'll do once I catch him. The sky is getting darker, turning purple, and I hear James call to us, "I see one, guys. I see a bat," but we are a ways away now. The lights from the tennis courts pop on, throwing shadows all over the park.

I am close to Alex, only a few feet away, when he turns and says, "I bet you can't kiss me." I am startled but say, "Bet I can." We are moving farther away from James and I wonder if he is worried. I gain on Alex easily and when I am close enough I lift him up into my arms and I can hear him giggling a low, heavy giggle, which vibrates through me like a hymn. I flip him over so he is lying in my arms. He is still giggling when I lean down and carefully kiss his forehead. It is a humid night and his skin is coated in a soft layer of moisture. He smells like the grass. When I raise my head and look at him, he is quiet. He is looking at me hard. He is looking for something. I think to smile, to say something like you would to a small child, but I just stare back. Finally his eyes dart from mine and he points to the sky and says, "Is that one?" And in the next instant James calls to us, "Guys, come here, you're missing it."

WHAT THE BOYS WERE LIKE

We were making cookies and Alex kept eating the cookie dough. His father, trying to be smart, told him it was fine. In fact, he could eat as much of it as he wanted. I nodded, knowing exactly where James was going with this. We sat across from Alex at the secondhand kitchen table and followed every mouthful. Waiting. Alex kept eating. Another bite. A pound at least. He never did get sick. It was a bust. Somehow that kid would always beat the rules.

Caleb, on the other hand, stood on the edge of a brand new playground that had just been completed, right outside the caution tape, while his father and Alex played on the new equipment. James called to him, told him to come on, it was fine. They wouldn't get in trouble. But still, Caleb stood there, watching them swing and slide. He couldn't cross that boundary.

That's just the way they were.

NAPTIME

One day, when we were still getting to know each other, we all four rode our bikes to the farmers market and then over to the football stadium and then back to James's.

When I got back to my own home, I had to take a nap. It was so exhausting. There were so many questions, so many needs and problems that the boys couldn't solve themselves. The littlest thing— a drink of water—was the biggest thing. I just wanted to sit down somewhere with a book.

The truth is, I was a little afraid of them. They could be so loud and unpredictable or manipulative. Also, I was terrified of what it would mean to have them (and their mother) in my life long-term. It was a lot.

I told my therapist about this and she said, "Well, maybe don't move in together anytime soon." What is soon? How do you better prepare to live with two children who are not your own?

HIS LIFE WITH HER

Each time we go to his ex-wife's house, I recognize something from his life with her. The rugs are the same ancient indigo rugs he has in his house. On the wall is a small painting he has done. A larger one, reminiscent of his style, he assures me was done by a colleague—someone who once was a friend of both of theirs. When I meet these friends, they smile at me. They are glad to see him with someone and they tell him that, sometimes in private, sometimes while I am standing there. But I can see that I confuse them. I am the new woman. I am not the boys' mother. I am young. One woman announces that she asked the boys if they liked me—my motives suspect she goes to the source. She is happy to report they said yes.

The dishes are the same, probably from their wedding, split after the divorce. The albums—Richard Buckner, John Prine. It is eerie. It seems to me—because I did not see them divide—that these duplicate items have just shown up in both of their houses, as if they should be on one of those shows about long-lost twins who when discovered turn out to both be dentists and wear plaid. As if they are each, still, one half of the other.

One day I open up a photo album sitting on her coffee table and am shocked to see a photo of James and her in the delivery room moments after the birth of their second son. They both look so happy.

At night, in bed, I ask God to make me a bigger person.

FORCE OF WILL

I didn't want it to be true. Like a Greek god, I wanted him to have sprung forth from the earth, fully formed with no past to speak of. And at first, I tried to make that so. Once, I bullied him into telling me he had never loved Lori, his ex-wife. Afterward I felt sick and satisfied.

I told myself he had made a mistake. He had gotten impatient, waiting for me, and had gone and married the wrong person. It was a character flaw, but we would overcome that.

I have this book on narcissists. The first defining characteristic is an exaggerated sense of self-importance. Another is a belief that one is special and unique and can only be understood by other special people. A third is a tendency to be envious. I bought this book because I believed James to be a narcissist. It is called *Help! I'm in Love with a Narcissist.*

FALLING IN LOVE

Caleb and I are sitting on the couch watching TV, when without looking, without thinking, he reaches out and takes hold of my hand. A boy and a grown woman. I don't look at our hands, or at him, afraid of breaking the spell.

It is just as it once was with his father. The same quickening of my heart, my hand becoming sweaty, except this time it is my hand that covers his small, slim fingers. Has he held hands with other girls? At school, at recess? Or is it just me?

CONVERSATION OVERHEARD

"I was going to have a first date with this girl. The first date was going to be walking her dog. My friends, they said maybe that wasn't such a good idea. They said: What if you like the dog?"

BAKED BEANS

The first time we took the boys to meet my parents, my mother didn't know how to comport herself. She tried to gather us together for a photo, but the boys were distracted. "Go stand by your mom and dad," my mother directed. Caleb looked at her, began to walk toward us and mumbled, "That's not my mom." I don't think my mother knew what else to say—who was I anyway?

My brother's children had not yet been born and so here were her first "grandchildren." But it wasn't right; they weren't right. Still, she was trying very hard. She had put on her happy face.

Later, she would say, "We were surprised, your dad and I, that you had chosen someone with kids." I think she was trying to tell me she knew it wouldn't work out. That from the beginning she felt I was making the wrong decision. This is kind of the way my family is. Decisions are right or wrong. And life is made up of them—it is up to you to do it right.

That first evening was warm. The six of us sat around my mother's dining table—used for special occasions—eating hamburgers, corn on the cob, and baked beans. James watched to make sure nothing spilled on my mother's beige carpet while the boys filled up the room with stories about their mother. "My mom has long brown hair and a dog," Caleb said.

At the end of the meal, Caleb hadn't touched his beans. My brother and I had not been allowed to be picky eaters. I remember eating scallops, liver and onions, and cottage cheese, which looked just like the white worms I dug up in the garden.

In an instant, my mother saw this as her chance to exact some control. She said, "Before you can leave the table, you must try them." Caleb looked to his father, who nodded.

Caleb put one lonely bean on his fork. "Good job," my mother said. We were all watching.

He put the bean to his lips and before it even made it to his tongue he burst into tears. He couldn't have played it better. Suddenly my mother felt horrible. She felt protective. She wanted to comfort. She brought out the dessert. And that was that.

The thing is, before that weekend was over the boys started calling my parents Grandma Dona and Grandpa Phil—unprompted. From then on they were never anything else. They say kids adapt better than adults to change. Or maybe it just doesn't hit them until much, much later.

MY MOTHER

My mother is the kind of woman who washes the garage floor with soap. She is the kind of woman who attends a regular Bible study. When it came to being a parent she read books like, *How to Really Love Your Child*, and the sequel, *How to Really Love Your Teenager*.

There wasn't one about loving your adult child. That was harder for her. Not that she didn't love me—just she wasn't exactly sure how to do it. She knew how to be the mother: how to make sure my sheets were freshly laundered and that I flossed my teeth regularly. When my brother was in high school, she once made a cheesecake for him to take on a picnic that was a date with a girl. That was when things started to get weird.

And me, what was I to do with her motherly example? There wasn't much I could use in my situation. I wanted to. I wanted to be the mother she had modeled. Maybe that was part of the problem.

MEMORY

On *Science Friday,* Steve Ramirez of MIT explains how we think of memory like a tape recorder. We think we can replay it just as it happened. But it is not like that at all. He calls it a "reconstructive process." Every time we remember something we must recreate the memory and that can change it. He says that you might insert new knowledge into a memory.

On the program, which I am listening to while making lunch on a Friday in my apartment in Chicago on the most beautiful August day, coolish and blue, they decide that the most accurate memories are in fact the ones we never think of.

THE DEEP SOUTH

James was doing an artist's residency in Alabama in the middle of summer. It was not just the South, but the Deep South. Train cars in muted rusts and blues traveled past the small town every hour. They looked hungry and lost.

One of the locals, who was connected with the studio where James was working, had just had his stomach stapled and couldn't eat fried food; he recommended we try the fried catfish at the local bar on his behalf. In the evenings we played euchre with the couple who ran the residency—who also happened to be James' former students. In the nights we made love in a whitewashed room as a window air conditioner hummed along.

At the end of his stay, James did a workshop and taught us all how to use the sun to make the prettiest deep blue prints you ever saw. It was like looking up at the sky from underwater.

GOSSIP

We move to Kentucky because James is offered a lectureship at the University there. I will be adjuncting at the same university. The boys stay behind with their mother, three hours away.

When we arrive, our neighbors greet us as we unload the truck. We have chosen a small bungalow on a quaint street—the only rental. Right away our neighbors say how glad they are that we are moving in, glad to have a nice, young couple in the house and both of us working down at the University. It is like they have won the lottery.

We get an earful about the last renters. Something shady was going on, too many UPS deliveries. And it must be true, because one evening there is a knock on the door and it's a police officer asking for some woman. When he is convinced I am not her and we don't know her, he speaks into a walkie-talkie and his partner comes around from his post in the back. They expected me to make a break for it.

The gay couple has a crush on James. Vegetables just show up on our doorstep. Around the corner is a small market that sells "hot lunch" composed of meatloaf and two sides. We feel we have won the lottery, too, eating homemade mac and cheese from Styrofoam containers.

Except, it is the first time James has ever lived away from his sons. Despite the hot lunch, he can't be happy. He lays silent on the couch for hours, impervious to my pleas, which only makes them louder.

But first I make sure the windows are shut. We want those vegetables to keep coming.

SELF-HELP I

A tip from *Two Happy Homes: A Working Guide for Parents & Stepparents after Divorce and Remarriage* by Shirley Thomas.

Practice active listening.

Example:
Child's Stepmother: The kids have been acting like monsters.
You: You seem to be pretty irritated with them.
Child's Stepmother: I'm about at the end of my rope.
You: I imagine you're quite frustrated.
Child's Stepmother: I am! I'm not used to so much noise and commotion all day.
You: I think I know what you're going through. They can be a handful.
Child's Stepmother: Thanks for understanding.

YOU MUST BE GOOD AT TRIVIA

Oh no, I'm not. That is not how my brain works. If you ask me what the woman's name was in that movie, I'll tell you that she was a blond and she wore a green bathing suit and she was in that other movie, you know the one with the blue cover, I think it had a lake on it. It will turn out not to be a lake though—it will be a public fountain.

I remember impressions of things, how things felt, not the details. For example, I can tell you when something happened based on what I remember about the weather. But, if it was an unseasonably cold day in June, I'll probably tell you it happened in October. Sometimes it is handy, like I can describe the way my grandmother's farm smelled: aged wood and sewage and cooked meat. But nobody ever wants to know that. They want to know the woman's name in that movie.

You've been warned.

THE SIX OF US

In the car one night on our way home from somewhere, Caleb announced that he thought I should marry his new stepdad, Ian, and James should remarry his mom and then all six of us should live together in one house. I could see how this made sense to him. His stepdad and I were in the same category—in his mind, we were the same. And I was flattered: Caleb hadn't discounted his stepdad and me. Even if his parents got back together, he imagined we were there to stay. As it turned out, that was not the case.

THIS IS NOT MY STORY TO TELL

Ian—Lori's new husband—died. While he was visiting friends on the West Coast for Christmas, there was a house fire. It was nighttime. Everyone was asleep. They say he woke up and called out, rousing the rest of the house, who all got out in time. But then he got disoriented with all the smoke and couldn't find the door.

IT WAS LIKE A DREAM

The first thing James tells me when we wake up—after sleeping on a futon in the basement of his ex-wife's new house because I refuse to sleep in her bed—is about his dream. There was a man outside pounding at the window, he says. In the dream, he thinks that he will fight the man if he needs to, but first James must lift his head from the pillow. When he does, he awakes to find that no one is there.

He tells me this as we prepare the boys for their last day of school before Christmas break. Lori and Ian have already left for the holiday—however not together. They are celebrating separately for logistical reasons. After school, James and I plan to pick up the boys and drive to my parents' home.

The call comes while we are out to breakfast. James stands up, walks to the middle of the restaurant, puts his hand on someone else's table to steady himself. They notice. He doesn't. I assume it is about Alex—too much red and green food dye—what has he done now? But it isn't. It's about Ian.

That's the first we hear.

The problem is, no one knows how to contact Lori. She hadn't told anyone exactly where she was going. Perhaps Ian had known. People thought James would know, but he doesn't, which is something in itself.

Things started moving then, fast and unsteady, like they do in a crisis. So I forgot to ask James how he felt. Because, it seems he was the last one to see Ian alive.

Was he standing at the window trying to get out of that other house or into his own? I'm sure he meant to come to Lori, but forgot that we were staying there instead. Did he realize that the man he came to as he was dying had in fact, upon occasion, wished him dead? Because I know James had—when Ian made the boys laugh or on a Tuesday when he knew Ian was there with them and James was not, when James felt him taking his place.

DON'T TELL

Lori didn't want us to tell the boys. She wanted to tell them. Later. So we told them there had been an accident, and Ian was in the hospital, sick. And that was true. He was on life support waiting for everyone to come and say goodbye. But the boys knew something more was wrong, because James and I both kept crying, at odd moments, at the McDonalds where we stopped for Happy Meals and root beers as we drove across Indiana and Illinois and into Iowa. When "Silent Night" played on the radio. When we looked at each other for too long. When we looked at the boys for too long.

Lori called and wanted the boys to talk to Ian, to say whatever they had to say to him. The boys were confused. Caleb went first. He said hello and waited for a response. We told him to just keep talking. So he talked about what he was hoping to get for Christmas. Then he said goodbye and waited. Nothing. He handed the phone to Alex, who was even more confused and just kept saying "Ian? Ian? Ian?"

Later, James felt guilty for not telling the boys it would be the last time they would ever talk to Ian. I didn't make him feel any better. I said, yes, we should have done that. I said that Lori needed to tell them, or let us tell them. Even in that moment, I thought how if I was the mother I would do things differently.

THE WOMEN IN THE FAMILY

During the memorial service, Lori sat with Ian's family. She had asked us to keep the boys, but Alex was hard to hold down. He wanted to go to his mother. After he squirmed and shifted and made a fuss, we let him go.

Lori was dressed in white like a jilted bride. And when I looked over at her, holding Alex on her lap, she was looking back at me. "I need you to take him," she mouthed across the aisles. "I need your help."

I read this essay once, about how a hummingbird's heart is so tiny. It can beat up to 1,260 times per minute. The heart aflutter. And then there is the whale, whose heart is like a room. A closet maybe. Maybe just the size of the attic under the eaves in the Old Country House. Yes, probably about that size for all the stuff tucked away there. My tiny bird heart had been clipping along and then I was standing in it.

Alex came back to sit with us. Lori read her eulogy about how she was angry with Ian for dying and about how the color white kept showing up and she took that as a sign—white flowers unexpectedly blooming on a house plant, the dress, the snow. Later that night, in the bathroom of the bar where they were having a celebration of life, Lori told me she loved me.

I guess some whales mate with the same partner for years, six years maybe. But not for life. That is a myth. Meanwhile, females always travel together. They help each other, assisting with births and ensuring newborns reach the surface of the water for air.

MEMORIAL

In the order of service at the memorial and in the newspaper articles, it reads: "Ian Williams leaves behind a wife and two sons. A memorial fund has been established to help his family during this difficult time." In a split second James is erased. After the service, acquaintances of Ian's say they didn't realize he had kids. They feel so silly. It makes sense, though. He was such a fun, goofy guy.

Ian, who was a musician with a band that had just started to get some notice, becomes more than local news. The story of his death, and his widowed young family, is everywhere.

Lori doesn't like the word "step," she says. She never has. They never used it. Is it too much, James asks, for a small word to be inserted so his sons remain his sons? She tells him it is. She tells him, full of despair, that Ian was the real father. James doesn't see despair. He sees his own faults in those words and he can hardly keep himself from choking her. A man whose hands still lift Caleb up for a kiss and whose hands reach for me with gentle ease. His hands, at his sides, think of what it would be like to stop those words right in her throat, to crush them before they formulate. Like an animal, he reminds her, he is the real father.

STEOP

Astieped: bereaved in Old English
becomes
Steopan: to bereave
becomes
Steop bearn: an orphan child, bereft of one or both parents

A *stepfather* might be considered one who becomes a father to a fatherless child, and a *stepson* an orphan who becomes a son by the marriage of the surviving parent.[1]

The earliest recorded use of the prefix *steop-* to denote familial connections is from the Corpus Gloss, an 8th century glossary of Latin-Old English words. The glossary includes the words *steopmoder, steopfaeder, steopsunu*.

Bereave: to deprive, rob, strip, dispossess, mostly of immaterial possessions like *life and hope*.

Steopfaeder: hopeless father
Steopsunu: deprived son

---

1. OED

German grammarian Johann Christoph Adelung believed that *stief*, the Dutch equivalent, signified something not genuine, in opposition to the genuine and true, but he confessed that from the great antiquity of this word derivation is very difficult.[2]

Stiefmoeder: untrue mother

Filiaster: The term *filiaster* occurs with reasonable frequency in epitaphs from the second century A.D. onwards. It is generally defined as the everyday equivalent of stepson or stepdaughter. Not all scholars, however, have regarded *filiaster* as an exact synonym. P. Meyer included *filiaster* in his discussion of terms employed to denote a child born from an illegitimate relationship.[3]

Foster-, Festermodor: a woman who cares for a child not her own.[4]

Fester.

Fester.

Fester: Of a wound or sore; to become a fester, to gather or generate pus or matter, to ulcerate.

Festermodor: A woman gathering pus.

---

2. Joseph Bosworth, *A Dictionary of the Anglo-Saxon Language* (Cambridge: Metcalfe and Palmer, Printers, 1836), 352.

3. "Filiaster: Privignus or 'Illigitimate Child'?" *Classical Quarterly* 39 (1989): 536-548.

4. Charles D. Campbell, *The Names of Relationship in English: a contribution to English semasiology* (Strassburg: Heitz & Mundel, 1905), 85.

GOOD DAYS

The ice is thinning on the small pond in Blue Limestone Park. Alex and I are helping Mother Nature spur on spring. With large rocks we smash through the ice and watch the water bubble up through the hole. Water so cold it could suffocate you.

We have finally made it out of the house. Both misfits. Both home in the middle of the day on a Wednesday. Alex has been asked to take a break from school. He is not expelled or suspended; the teachers just need a break.

He has been labeled "difficult." The evidence: he punched the principal in the stomach (which is where he could reach). He told a kid on the bus that he had a knife, even though he didn't. When the bus driver came back to investigate Alex stuck to his story, so the police were called along with all of the other parents who had to come pick up their children.

Me? I am without work. We have moved again—to Ohio—this time James has landed the whale: a tenure-track job. We celebrated as if it was our joint career, but I now have little to do. After a lot of trial and error, I have finally come to understand why people like soap operas.

There is a small hole open in the middle of the pond. And while we watch, two geese fly in and land in perhaps the only open water for miles. We are both silent. The geese preen, swimming small circles around each other. Alex is breathing slowly—I know because I can see the white plume as he exhales.

"I'm thinking of an animal," he says. "It starts with the letter T."

"Tiger?" He shakes his head. "Tarantula?" Nope. The geese are bobbing their heads under the water now, looking for food. I know the answer. Alex is thinking of the tapir—an animal he likes to choose to stump us. I guess a few more before bringing up the tapir. At first he says no, that isn't it. But then slowly he admits I have guessed it. I reach out to tickle him and he in turn jumps on me and we wrestle to the ground. After a while we lay side by side, looking up at the sky, panting. We watch the geese fly on.

Years later, when I am at a zoo and see a tapir—long snout, big droopy eyes, ugly as sin—I am shocked. Honestly, I didn't think it really existed.

SPELL

On Fridays I would go get the boys from their mother—driving in the bright afternoon sun from our state to theirs.

I would park at a gas station and wait. This was the transfer spot. When Lori and the boys arrived, it didn't take long. The boys slid from the backseat of one car to the other, carrying their backpacks, heads down staring at their PSPs, saying "Hey, Paula." Alex would look out the window and follow his mother's car as she drove off, then return to his game.

Back on the road, it took the boys a little while to adjust—to remember how this goes. But soon Caleb would look up and say, "What movies did you get?" On Friday mornings I would stop by our library and comb through the movies, trying to find some that I thought the boys might like. *White Fang*, *Rudy*, *Spaceballs*. I chose things that I had once loved. That is one of the privileges of caring for children.

"Let's watch this," Caleb said to Alex, choosing *Rudy*. "Okay," Alex said, putting his thumb in his mouth and kicking off his shoes, releasing the faint smell of mildew. In the rear view mirror, I watched them watch the portable DVD player—which we had bought on sale just for this purpose. They laughed together. They were concerned together. "What does that mean, Cal?" Alex asked. Ahead were the open plains of the Midwest and neat little strip malls composed of Walmarts and Dairy Queens.

They were only allowed one movie—that was my rule. The last hour was screen-free. Caleb would quiz me from the world atlas: "What is the capital of Kazakhstan?" We would play Eye Spy. They would fight. Often they would ask me to tell them a story, "Tell us about when you were a kid."

On these drives we became a unit. As we neared home it would be nighttime and Alex would be getting sleepy. I could have kept going.

When we got home, James would be waiting and the boys would forget their backpacks in their excitement to greet him—running from the car to his arms. I would stay behind, picking up the fast food wrappers and gathering Alex's shoes for when he would need them in the morning.

PARENTHOOD

Alex had pinworms. He couldn't stop scratching his butt. James had to take a flashlight and go into his room under the cover of darkness and quickly shine the light on Alex's backside. The pinworms had to be taken by surprise.

James did this without complaint and in all seriousness. Alex was embarrassed and uncomfortable—I shouldn't even be telling you this now. We didn't talk about it when he was around. Still, I sterilized everyone's sheets and all the counters, just to be sure.

When I asked James to clean the bathroom, he got squeamish. He would call on me to clean grease out of a pan left overnight. He didn't have a strong constitution. But without hesitation he inspected his son for worms.

WWE

While lying in bed, James wondered aloud how many professional wrestlers we could name.

"John Cena," I said.

"Big Show," he said.

"CM Punk," I said.

"The Undertaker," he said.

"MVP," I said.

"Randy Orton," he said.

This went on for a while. Then we laughed and laughed. We were both artists. At first James wasn't sure what it meant that *his* children were so obsessed with professional wrestling. What did it signify? But, he had given in. It was what the boys talked about. So it was good that we had studied up.

BLENDED FAMILY

We think it's all so new and uncertain and most likely damaging but also potentially beautiful. The modern family. Stepsiblings and half-siblings and grandpa's new girlfriend. Currently, four out of 10 people consider themselves to be part of a blended family.

For the last half-century headlines have been shouting about the family's demise. This is always the case with humans, though. Every generation thinks it will usher in the end of the world. How could the world keep going without us, after all? But, sometimes it is good to remind ourselves that we are not so special.

I picked up the book *Marriage, a History* by Stephanie Coontz and found myself amused at the elaborate ways families have been arranged and rearranged—ghost marriages and wife loaning are both actual terms. Then in the chapter "Soap Operas of the Ancient World" she mentions Octavia—wife to Mark Antony—and I'm no longer amused.

We are always the same, us humans. We think we progress, but that is only in external accouterment.

OCTAVIA

Octavia, Octavia. What kind of woman you must have been. Eight children to watch over, five your own, one from your husband's first marriage and two the product of his long love affair. He died in her arms, as history would tell again and again. And you, you were left to care for the children.

Your beauty was said to surpass even hers. So, what did she have that you did not? You must have wondered. A kingdom I suppose. And her ability to stare right back at her own teeth marks once she had taken a bite, while you stood solemnly in your kitchen, a pillar of feminine virtues. How it burned. What did they call you, those children? Did they taunt you behind your back? Or were you all of one piece, left behind in dull-witted love's irresponsible wake?

But let's be honest. You didn't give the choicest cut of meat to Cleopatra's son. Why would you? At night, by the fire, you never held them in your lap. How could you? You had teeth and they left marks. But you were better bred. You knew how to place them so no one else could see.

LONELY TOGETHER

It's lonely. That's something you don't expect. It doesn't seem that if you have a fiancé and two almost stepchildren that it will be lonely. But it is. Not silent lonely, loud lonely. When the boys were around there was plenty of noise and yelling and talk and energy. But, I was always just a little outside of it. When we played games, the three of them took turns reinforcing their allegiance to each other. I'd get overly competitive, trying to prove my place.

When the boys weren't around it was silent lonely, James second-guessing all his decisions.

I told James that it was important that in the larger scheme of things our relationship be the primary one, and he agreed that made sense. But that's not how it had been built. For all of them, I would always be secondary, coming into their lives long after their own bond had been solidified. It was like trying to run in a dream. You keep thinking you're going to create some momentum and get somewhere, but there you stand.

MISSING NOTES

Oh mother, I have begun to sing. I have begun to sing on car trips with my partner's sons who sit in the back and ask me to stop. Which I don't. I sing while doing housework, cleaning floors and counters. And when I recognize some forgotten tune hijacked by the television, I let my voice ring out. Not to be stopped. Not to be interrupted. Just a moment, just a moment, I'm singing.

I sing songs I hardly know, missing words or notes, but that doesn't stop me, as I remember it never stopped you, mother. My songs are strange ditties that I hear in your voice, having never heard any proper arrangement. The tunes and the words come straight from your mouth mother, as if you were a bird regurgitating them into my beak and now I am spitting them back up, looking for my own young to feed.

I know why now, why you sang while doing the dishes, while driving the car, while putting on your cold cream, right up around your vibrating throat. As I lift my voice above the silence, I know how it feels to send out a message in song to those around you who seem to be deaf. You try to hit a note so high it can penetrate your own heart, which has also been deafened.

KELLEYS ISLAND

We went camping on Kelleys Island off Lake Erie. Just James and me, which was unusual. We were newly engaged.

We had to take the car ferry. We got out of our station wagon and walked around the big, lumbering boat. It was late on a Friday in fall and I was so excited I kept clapping.

We learned later that every year a circus comes to the island and carts over elephants and camels on the ferry. I thought that was magnificent.

We set up our tent right next to the water on the north side of the island. We couldn't believe no one else had snatched up those spots. Then the wind started blowing and we understood better. While making hot dogs, we had to yell to be heard.

"Get the ketchup out of the cooler in the backseat."

"What?"

"The ketchup."

"What?"

The wind kept pushing our words aside.

The next day we took a tour of the island and came upon some strange-looking birds. Black with a curved neck and little squat legs. I had my bird book, but before I could reach for it James said, "They're cormorants." That seemed implausible to me, mainly because it was not normally the kind of stuff he knew. But he was right. Dead on. Strange how after all that time, someone can still surprise you. The cormorant.

That night we went out to dinner at one of the few restaurants on the island. James wanted to talk about the boys coming to live with us most of the time. Again he was right; it was something we needed to discuss, but not then.

Not when we were on the island with the cormorants. Not when I might see a tiger cross the lake on a ferry. Not then. Not then.

MY MOTHER SLEW ME, MY FATHER ATE ME

AN ANNOTATED VERSION OF AN OLD FAIRY TALE[1]

When the woman looked out the window and saw the boy walking home, it was as if the devil had taken hold of her. The little boy walked in the door, and the devil got her to whisper sweetly to him and say: "My son, would you like an apple?" Then she looked at him fiercely.[2]

"Stepmother," said the little boy, "how angry you look. Yes, give me an apple."[3]

---

1. Original story from *The Annotated Classic Fairy Tales*, edited with an introduction and notes by Maria Tatar, 2002.

2. She looked at him this way because he never ate apples. In fact, the only thing he ever did eat was white bread and pasta. She anticipated a struggle.

3. This is not what the boy said. The boy said: "I *hate* apples. What else is there? Can't I have a Pop Tart?" The boy's father loved Pop Tarts, so there were some in the cupboard. And she would rather have given him the Pop Tart, because she hated struggling over food. She thought that if he was her own child she would have told him he had to have an apple before he could have anything else and that would have been that.

When the little boy bent down into the apple chest, the devil prompted her and bam! She slammed the lid down so hard that the boy's head flew off and fell into the chest.[4] Then she was overcome with fear and thought: "How am I going to get out of this?"[5]

But it wasn't that easy with her stepchild because there were rules from two houses and she needed the child's father to establish this first, which he didn't really want to do because the kid was only there on weekends so he wanted him to have a good time and Pop Tarts were part of that. She was certain she could have been more firm with her own child and she would have set up these rules long ago. Setting up rules long ago were the sort of things of her daydreams.

4. No, no. She was not a violent person. She often felt a deep urge to throw her coffee cup against the wall, but even that she never did do.

5. This thought was not about the boy at all. It was a general thought about her life situation and usually it was more along the lines of "How did I get here?" She could feel herself slowly shrinking, like Alice in Wonderland. She knew it was partly her fault. Her partner was always telling her she needed to be more assertive. If she had felt that way she should have let him know. She was not very good at being assertive, except at the wrong moments when she just couldn't take it anymore so she just blurted something out too blunt and too strong and ended up feeling bad herself for saying whatever it was she had said.

She had told him once that she hated the boy. It wasn't really the boy she hated, though. It was just that he was there and disrupted her idea of what her life should look like and also he took so much of her partner's attention and there was the ex-wife and everything was so complicated that she ended up with a stomachache. Her partner's therapist had said to let her express whatever feelings she had. So she had told her partner she hated the boy. And her partner let her say it. But he never forgot it. Even after he knew that she actually loved the boy. He never forgot it and it was one of those things she could never take back.

She took the little boy and chopped him up. She put the pieces into a pot and cooked them up into a stew.[6]

When the father came home, he sat down at the table and said: "Where's my son?"[7]

Then he began to eat. And eat. And eat.

---

6. Whoever was translating this story really got it wrong. She had never had one fantasy about chopping the boy up and putting him in a stew. What is more likely is that they made a stew together, her and the boy. It turned out the boy liked to cook and she liked to cook with him. He was a good student and they could turn on music. He was also so pleased with whatever he made that he would eat it, or at least try some of it.

7. This part is true. The boy's father could never stop thinking about him, which was sweet. Everyone loved this, because all he wanted was to be a good father. Even when she and her partner took trips, just the two of them, he talked a lot about the boy. And when they were supposed to have a night out, if the phone rang and it was his ex-wife, he always picked up. It could be an emergency after all. Which she understood. But really, by the end, she thought that there should be some time, at least some time, when it was just the two of them. He got angry then and said things like: "You have me every night of the week; he is only here a few days out of the month." But that was a big lie. She didn't have him those nights. Nobody did.

A METAPHOR FOR SOMETHING

The landing for my next, booted step: a thick, red centipede moving slowing across the dirt path. Tiny black flies congregate on its back, driving it crazy. It squirms and bucks then rolls up into a spiral as perfect as a galaxy. The flies disperse. But when it starts out again it seems to have lost its way. Going in no purposeful direction, it marches on and the flies return. It squirms and bucks then rolls up into a spiral as perfect as a galaxy. The flies disperse. But when it starts out again it seems to have lost its way. Going in no purposeful direction, it marches on and the flies return. It inches farther this time, determined to endure, before it must squirm and buck then roll up into a spiral as perfect as a galaxy. When it starts out again it seems to have lost its way.

MAGIC

James has this story about one of the first times we met. This was when we didn't really know each other. So far, all we had done was smile at one another obsessively. The story goes that he was getting a ride somewhere from a friend and he saw me across the street and he told his friend to stop, to pull over, because he wanted to talk to that girl. That girl, he says. The friend didn't understand him and so they just drove on by, James waving as they went, calling *hello* out the window. James thought there was something funny about it, something poetic.

The thing is—and I never told him this—I had been following him. I had watched him leave his office then walked behind him a few paces around the corner and down the street to his friend and his friend's car. I had been hoping (and worrying) that he would see me, that we might say a few words, that he would be reminded of me. When I went to the grocery store I wondered if I would run into him. He must grocery shop, right? He would have to go to the grocery store at some point.

This was when he was still a blank slate. He was everything I imagined him to be and nothing that I couldn't handle. They say our first impression of someone is what matters. It takes many, many encounters to change a first impression.

We all have our stories about when we start loving someone. If done right, they are a kind of sleight of hand with the eye only catching what the heart wants it to see.

OUR FAULTS

We had our faults. Once, James didn't talk to me for eight hours on a long car trip. We sat side by side. The reason was unclear. He didn't say one word. Once, I admonished him over dinner for all of the ways I felt he was failing and left him there with his head in his hands, plate untouched, while I went to take a bath. More than once, James outright ignored me. Once, when James was ignoring me, I threw a plastic bowl to get his attention.

We were both Midwesterners; a grave look or a well-placed silence might as well have been a knife held to the throat.

HIDDEN LIFE

The sea monkeys were Caleb's. They had come in a package deco-
rated with cartoon drawings of the crustaceans, all smiling with
three antennae each. "INSTANT LIFE," the package said. Caleb
was gone, at his mother's, so I was tending them in his absence.
Their plastic container sat on the windowsill in the living room,
which was cold and drafty in February. I fed them a scoop of the
salt-like food, looked closely and decided they were duds. We had
yet to see any sea monkeys.

These were a boy's adventure. The inventor of the sea monkey,
Harold von Braunhut, originally sold them through the mail from
ads in comic books. He also sold X-Ray Specs and invisible gold-
fish (non-existent fish that were guaranteed to remain invisible). I
wondered if our sea monkeys had somehow gotten mixed up with a
package of invisible fish.

But the next day, I went into the living room and there they
were—graceful and airy, dancing around, to and fro. It was late

afternoon and the winter sun falling to the west caught the translu-
cent creatures just so. It felt like I was witnessing a miracle. I wanted
someone else to confirm it, but no one was around. I lay down on
the couch and watched them until the sun began to sink behind the
neighbor's house.

The sea monkey is actually a brine shrimp. Brine shrimp are
one of the few organisms that experience cryptobiosis—a response
to adverse environmental conditions when all metabolic processes
stop and the organism goes into a dormant state. In that state it can
live indefinitely, waiting for conditions to improve. When they do, it
pops back to life. The term cryptobiosis means *hidden life*. A miracle,
essentially.

I so wished Caleb was there to see it.

SELF-HELP II

Perusing self-help books I find this in *How to Be a Good Stepmom* by S.T. Casey Celia with "Over 40 hints, tips and pieces of advice!"

Do: Remember at all times that you are an adult.

Don't: Revert to childish ploys to get attention from your husband and away from the children.

There is probably no single faster way to alienate your husband and the children than to make him choose sides. This is unhealthy for all concerned. Entering into any marriage is for adults only! There is no room in the stepparenting role for game playing, except in your living room with your family—board and dice!

TENDER

It was the end of summer. Cicadas still made their panicked, trilling noises from the trees. A week later I would need a jacket to go out and get the mail. James and the boys and I were playing football. I had never even understood football until I met Caleb, who took the time to explain it step by step while he watched whatever game was on.

While we were playing, I misjudged the arch of the ball and it caught me right on the tip of my pointer finger. My finger bent back so hard tears came to my eyes. I had to sit down. I had to hold my finger against my chest and breathe slowly.

James laughed. He was angry. We both were. Things had come to pass. He laughed and so the boys laughed. And I knew then: there was no more tenderness between us.

PINK LADY'S SLIPPER

James teaches me the name of the Pink Lady's Slipper—a delicate flower growing in the ditch. Just a tiny puff of pink. Look fast, or you'll miss it. The flower is an anomaly among the ditch weeds; its whole life a surprise.

The week the Lady's Slipper blooms is not a good week. I feel like I am being broken open from the inside, like the threads of the fungus that push their way inside the flower's seeds until they burst. Every time I leave the house to run some errand I see the pink standing stalwart and I think of James saying, offhanded, "That's rare," which leads to me thinking about other things he's said that are harder to stomach.

At one point I am driving off to the grocery store and I see the Lady's Slipper and it makes me feel desperate, like I will die if I don't hear him tell me one more time about the flower. So I call him at his studio and simply say, "I just passed the Lady's Slipper," and he does not realize it is an offering, a plea, a last attempt. He doesn't say any of the things I want him to say. He says, "Oh, Paula."

This is the week I tell a friend that I am afraid that I might be one of those brides who just doesn't show up on the day of her wedding and the friend says, "You know, you don't have to get married." Somehow that is the permission I need. We decide to postpone the wedding. It seems everyone besides us knows what that really means.

After that week, the Pink Lady's Slipper is gone, back into the earth.

THE MANATEE EXHIBIT

We stand at the Columbus Zoo with the rest of the crowd and stare at the manatees. The two animals are both female and they rest on their backs on the bottom of their pool, stomachs exposed, gigantic and cartoon-like. The sign next to me says, "Manatees may be the origin of the mermaid myth." I point this out to James and we smile because the myth has strayed so far. They each weigh over a thousand pounds. They each have small front flippers and a tail like an anvil. They each seem impossible, make-believe, and so I guess, like mermaids.

James wants to take my picture up against the glass. He positions me and snaps. We have come to the zoo in a moment of mania. So when the woman at the ticket booth explains that a one-year membership would only cost twenty dollars more, we go for it, giddy, defying what we left at home, the cold eggs overdone, the yard full of dead leaves, the moving van that will come in one week and that I will load by myself leaving our bed for him, even though I know he won't sleep in it. "You could always stay," he says. "I mean, you're going to want to take advantage of this membership." We both joke because otherwise we can't say what might happen, looking in at these mermaids.

One of the animals, named Holly, looks at the crowd. The sign says, "Manatees have advanced long-term memories." What is she remembering, I wonder? She floats to the surface to breathe. Tips her nose above the water, a small blip, while below is the body of a giantess. I imagine she is remembering the sailors she has wooed, dark water at night, her children. I imagine she is remembering sorrow or a secret from her beginnings, 45 billion years ago. I imagine she is remembering something we have forgotten, something we know we have forgotten, but as hard as we try, still cannot recall.

THE TABLE

I had purchased the kitchen table a few years before James and I moved in together. It was the only brand new piece of furniture I had ever bought. Otherwise it was used futons and secondhand lamps.

A week after we decided to end things, James and I went to the grocery store for something simple, like milk. It was late. We needed to leave the house. Neither one of us wanted to be home alone.

On the way I mentioned something about the table; I don't even know what or how it came up. But whatever it was, I made it clear I would be taking it with me when I left.

Perhaps that was the moment when it felt the most final. Perhaps it was too concrete—imagining the empty space left behind. Whatever it was, James couldn't take it. His voice went low and dark.

"No. If you're leaving us fine, but I get the table. I'm keeping that table."

I was shocked. The table wasn't that fancy and wasn't worth much. It was made of pine.

"It's my table," I said. "I'm taking the table. Why do you even want it?"

"You can do what you want, but you don't get to just take our fucking table."

It seems kind of absurd now. People usually fight over houses and stock options. But I guess it isn't the item that matters.

When we got to the grocery store I went inside and James stayed in the car. There was some outdoor furniture on display and I sat down in one of the chairs and didn't get up. I sat there for half an hour and stared at the florescent lights overhead. The place was deserted. Like I said, it was late.

Eventually James came in to find me and said I should take the table. It was hard for him to say. Not because he was mad at that point, but because he knew he was giving in to it all.

It would take James a long time to get a new table. He wasn't great at the everyday stuff. They'd be eating on the couch for weeks. The moving van was slated to come the Monday before Thanksgiving. I imagined James and Caleb and Alex eating Thanksgiving dinner on the couch.

The next day I went to Goodwill and bought them a table for $40.

I took mine with me. I still have it.

CUPCAKES

Four cupcakes. Vanilla and chocolate with frosting like the sea and little pink orchids laid carefully afloat on the top. They look like miniature wedding cakes. Alex says he wants the chocolate one. His brother shoots him a look and his mother instructs him to let me choose first. He obliges without complaint. I choose the vanilla.

When I take the first bite, my tongue wants to expel the sugary cake so thick with butter it is like pure fat. But I don't. Instead, I take another bite. It is important that this be a significant moment and eating the cupcake that Caleb and Alex have chosen for me on the occasion of my departure is part of that.

I think of them all standing together at the bakery counter, on their way home from school, picking out the cupcakes. I know the boys insisted on the delicate ones, the girly ones, because I am a girl. Once, James let the boys choose what to get me for my birthday: a purse or a bike. Under 10 years old and they went with the purse.

James's ex-wife is making a gesture. She is doing her job as the mother. Who would have thought this too would fall to her? She is bearing it with grace.

My car is waiting right outside. It is late afternoon, just like the many times I have made this long drive to pick up the boys for the weekend. Perhaps we will all three get in the car and head home. Most likely we will all get carsick from the sweet cake and have to stop on the side of the road like the time I let them get ice cream from Bruster's.

When I leave, alone, I realize that this is probably the last time I will see them for a long time. I am heading off in the other direction to a place miles away.

I do not think it is the last time I will ever see them.

ACT II

SILENCE

There is no term for what I am. There are no instructions on how I am supposed to act towards Caleb and Alex. We have landed on the moon of relationships. My category is somewhere over there with gelding and born-again Jew. There is no way to make sense of it.

After I left, I called sometimes and sent gifts on holidays and birthdays. From miles away Alex said my name with a question: "Paula?" He said he was thinking of an animal that started with an S. I guessed Sasquatch, then spider, then spider monkey. He giggled. Then he said Caleb wanted to talk.

Caleb was playing on his PSP and narrated the game to me before saying he should probably go. He asked if I wanted to talk to his dad. I said no, I had called to talk to him. He held the phone away and yelled, "She doesn't want to talk to you." Which, at that moment, I didn't.

I hung up the phone and listened to the silence. A silence I had often craved when the boys were in the house.

Time as a child moves slowly. A year passes and it is like traveling to a distant star. The last time I talked to Caleb he said, "I haven't talked to you in *forever*." It had been a few months. To me it didn't seem so long. I wondered if I should call more often. But, I knew that I wouldn't.

After a while a friend suggested that maybe it would be better for everyone if I just stopped.

And so I did.

HOME

After all was said and done, I moved home to the small town where I had won the DAR Good Citizenship Award as a senior in high school. My mother had readied my room like a woman preparing a nursery. As I lay down to sleep, I could hear her sigh in relief: I had returned to her.

My mother once told me that the most satisfying time in her life had been when my brother and I were little. Her purpose so clear; our need so great. Now here I was, the child again.

Soon we fell into a rhythm that I had never been able to execute with my faux family. My parents were both retired and we ate all three meals together—breakfast, lunch and dinner. Clean up could not have been more efficient if it had been done by the Von Trapps.

In the evenings, my parents and I watched television. Each night they had a program or two they couldn't miss. My mother spoke of the characters as if she knew them. She pondered their motives. Then my father would ask if anyone wanted a drink. A brandy maybe, something with cranberry juice? And every night the choice would delight us—as if we were on vacation in the Alps.

Breakfast, lunch AND dinner was a bit much though.

IT PAINED ME TO DISAPPOINT HER

My hometown is in the middle of Illinois. It is surrounded by corn-fields and the whole bit. So when I entered the grocery store a couple weeks after moving in with my parents, I ran right into my second grade teacher. Mrs. Nelson. She was a kind woman, whom I loved. Standing six feet tall she towered over those 7-year-olds, and me, even now. She asked if I was home for a visit. She asked what I was doing, where was I living? She said, "You must be taking the world by storm." She actually said that: "You must be taking the world by storm." We were both leaning on our carts. I considered lying. It pained me to disappoint her—just as it had when I missed words on my spelling tests. Which I always did. Despite this fault, great things were still expected. But it was not turning out like we had all thought. After that I let my mother go to the grocery store. I couldn't take any more hopes dashed.

SMALL THINGS

It was a red fleece pullover. Good quality, featured on a rack amidst Carhartt coats at Farm & Fleet. My mother and I had gone to pick up some plant food. We also could have purchased some Goodyear tires or house paint, if we had felt so inclined. What I'm saying is the store was not known for its high fashion. But it looked so warm and also respectable. Good quality, like I said. My mother could tell that I was drawn to it. I tried it on, right over my clothes. I don't even think it was on sale. (My mother only buys things that are on sale.) That was right after I moved home. Because of the way things had worked out, I didn't have any money of my own then, which is like trying to only breathe in. At home, I set it on my dresser and kept touching it. The soft, downy feel. It smelled like tires. After everything else was gone, it was something to possess.

I still have it, but I think it's peculiar now. It is boxy and reserved. It is for a woman who is afraid of being naked.

DOCTOR'S ORDERS

I needed to refill a prescription for anti-depressants, so I went to a doctor in my hometown. I had never seen her before—but her name was familiar. There were only a few primary care physicians in town.

I sat in the exam room and waited. The walls were tooth enamel white. It was cold, January. I left my coat on. The doctor came in 20 minutes late looking down at my chart and asked me what I did for a living. I told her I was a writer. She wrote something down.

"How old are you?"
"31."
"Are you married?"
"No."

She looked up at me for the first time. "Why not?" she asked.

Why not? I wondered if she wanted me to tell her the whole story. Why not? Just, let me tell you why not. Why not? I started to cry.

My tears did not dissuade her.

"There are two things I have done in my life that I am glad for," she said. "I became a doctor and I had a daughter. If you want a family, you need to start thinking about that now."

Lots of women have stories along these same lines. It seems you hit a certain age and if you haven't checked off the right boxes on the forms, it becomes your doctor's responsibility to question your life choices.

But, from what I've heard, most doctors are more subtle. Usually they say things like, "I just want to make sure you have all of the information at your disposal so you can make the best choice for you." Then they proceed to tell you about fertility and how from here on out it just gets more dire.

Perhaps I did not look like a person who could detect subtlety.

The doctor went on. She told me about her own husband, who was a bit of a pushover. How on airplanes he always offered to help lift other people's luggage up into the overhead compartments. Which she thought was nice, but also irritated her. But all this was to say, he was fine. He was a good husband. Certainly, good enough. And when she had wanted to get married, there he was. And he had given her a daughter, who was in her late twenties and lived in New York and had recently ended a long-term relationship and who also needed to think more about where her life was going.

Ah, there it was. I had walked into that office on the wrong day—the day that I suddenly looked strikingly similar to this woman's daughter. And, unlike her daughter, I was a captive audience.

After her little speech someone knocked on the door, sorry to interrupt. The doctor was called away for a moment to attend to something.

I looked around the white room. There were cotton balls on the counter in a container with a silver lid. When I was a child I used to think they looked like candy. I thought for a moment about that child and all of the future paths that had been both ascribed to her and waiting inside of her.

Then I got up, opened the door and walked out.

WHITE SOCKS

I wouldn't let James turn his music up too loud and he wouldn't take any of my suggestions about how to arrange the furniture. I remember when I was young, in my early twenties, I knew this woman. She was divorced. She had dyed blond hair. She said something about someone who was wearing white socks with brown dress shoes. She said, "Maybe if my husband hadn't done that so much, maybe if he hadn't had so many damn white socks, we would still be married." That was the strangest thing I had ever heard. How could socks ruin a marriage? Now, I think perhaps they can. At least, when paired with everything else.

MOMENTUM

It's like a car crash. Not in the sense of a wreck and all that, but rather in the sense of physics: momentum and bodies in motion. There is an abrupt stop, but part of you can't help but keep moving in the direction you were already headed.

For at least a year after, every time I went to some event, I made a mental note about whether or not it would be a good venue for our wedding. I've heard it can be like this with great loss. There is a part of you that understands the truth and a part of you that doesn't. When someone dies, I've heard sometimes spouses keep that person's clothes for years, just in case they need them. When asked, they say they know it is irrational, but it doesn't matter. It is beyond rationality.

TRANSFERENCE

I'm playing with my nephew and all he wants to do is wrestle and climb on my back. He wants me to spin him around and around and then have us fall down together on the couch in a heap, dizzy and exhausted. He asks that we do that again and again, until I decide I am so tired it is dangerous to keep going. Then we lay together for a while on the couch. He points out the mole on my neck and keeps pushing at it, like it is a button.

His mother teases him, saying he has a crush. I am way beyond crush. I am totally in love. And I am thankful. Thankful for the weight of him in my arms. Thankful for the completely unreserved and unselfconscious way he gives of himself.

He has no idea all that he is for me.

DO YOU REMEMBER?

"Remember that dog, George?" I ask my brother.

"What dog?"

"When we were living on the canal? He was a yellow lab or something like that and he lived in the neighborhood. We named him George."

"Maybe, now that you mention it."

"Remember how we used to go out on the canal with our ice skates on and we'd give George one end of a stick and he'd pull us?"

"No, I don't remember that."

"You don't? He'd pull so fast. It was so much fun."

"I remember the ice skates though. Remember that we found them up in the attic of that house?"

"We did?"

"Yeah, they were in the attic."

"Did that place even have an attic?"

"Sure."

We are having this discussion while we are ice-skating with my niece. She has never been ice-skating before and is holding on tight. She has one hand in her father's, one in mine. She is five and she says, "That's funny. You remember one thing and you remember a different thing."

"That is funny," I say.

I am having a hard time believing that my brother doesn't remember, though. Once we thought George followed us to school because we saw a dog that looked just like him. We were distraught. We worried he couldn't find his way back home. We loved George. More than our own dog, who was small and white and got rashes on his pink skin that he licked and licked until it was raw. Or at least I did. Plus I'm pretty sure I owned my own skates by then. White figure skates with cotton laces.

I'm pretty sure.

RELIEF

"Were you relieved when you left or did you miss them?" The woman who asks me this is a mother of two children. She seems enamored with the prospect of just walking away. I say that I missed them. "But weren't you also relieved?" she asks. The truth is, I was. All that worry and negotiation, gone. Poof. No longer my concern. Like letting my fingers slip from the edge.

The woman has graying hair. Her two children are in their twenties. We have met briefly at a writing residency where she has the room next to mine. Through the walls, I can hear her talking on the phone to her husband. Later, she tells me he sang to her "You Are My Sunshine." They have a bond like that established between survivors of a hijacking. At one point she describes her daughter as "a terror," although the daughter is doing better now.

Then the woman looks at me and says, "There are benefits to not having children. Real benefits."

EUPHORIA

Once I started to get my life back together, I moved to Chicago and everything that happened thrilled me. I went out to brunch with a friend . . . brunch! Nothing had ever seemed so wonderful. I bought new shoes and couldn't get over them. I sat in the coffee shop and watched it rain outside the big front windows while jazz played on the radio. Every step I took felt like a luxury. Everything I bought— down to the baby carrots at Jewel—felt like a gift.

I knew this woman who got in a car accident. Her car flipped a couple times before landing on its top in the ditch. But she was fine. She climbed out the passenger-side window with nothing more than a few bruises. As she scrambled up the side of the ditch she said she started screaming, "I'm alive. I'm alive. I'm alive." A car stopped to help and the first thing she told the person was, "I'm alive."

BIRTH MOTHER

My cousin Elsie was adopted. When she was in her twenties she contacted the adoption agency asking for information about her birth mother. Turned out, her birth mother still lived in Rockford, Illinois—where Elsie knew she had been born. According to the records, the woman had been a girl, just 15, when she'd given birth. That was in the 1970s, right after Roe v. Wade. A woman's choice was the stuff of newspaper headlines. But when it came down to it, when it came down to one 15-year-old girl (and it always does come down to one) there probably wasn't much of a choice. What would she know to do? And so there was Elsie with her curly brown hair and the way she threw one foot out to the side slightly when she walked—not so much as to be a distraction, just enough to be adored.

Elsie wrote to her birth mother to tell her that she was doing well and had a good life. The woman's return letter was cordial. She was married and dropped some hints that suggested she had never told her husband about her first baby and she wasn't too keen on him finding out. The woman had a new daughter now, who was 12. She sent pictures of the new daughter riding her bike in a neighborhood in Rockford. After that, there wasn't much correspondence.

Later, Elsie was at a party and met a girl from Rockford. She said, in jest, feeling sure of herself in that outfit that she liked with a drink in her hand, "Oh I know Rockford. Do you know Linda Mansfield?" The girl smiled and said, "Of course, she's our neighbor. We went to her house for a barbeque just last week."

Elsie looked up at the girl, the stranger, who had been to a barbeque in Rockford, Illinois with her mother, just last week. Her mother, sitting in a lawn chair at a barbeque, holding a beer, telling her husband to check the burgers and talking to this girl. Her mother, who up until that moment had been invisible, hiding behind Elsie's own skin. She wanted to breathe in the girl, to capture some of the late summer evening Rockford air and hold it in her lungs as long as she could, before exhaling and smiling and telling the girl she didn't really know the woman, she was just an old friend of her mother's.

THAT'S NOT ALWAYS THE CASE

I was having this argument with a friend who said that biology wasn't a big deal when it came to families; it was all about psychology. I said that couldn't be the case. That flew in the face of everything I had read and all the Lifetime movies I had seen. Biology was a huge factor—in fact it was strange how much people felt connected to biological family members, like some invisible string held them together even across continents.

I cited a study that said people with step-relatives feel a stronger sense of obligation towards their biological family members. I didn't cite my own personal research—how while playing games with Caleb and Alex and James, they would pass the ball amongst themselves.

My friend said he had a stepfather, whom he loved just as much as his other family members. And a half-brother whom he never thought of as half at all.

I said that might be the case, but I had my own experiences and he couldn't argue with my truth.

To which he said, *Your truth is your truth, but my truth is* the *truth*. He had an attitude that way. Who could blame him, he had grown up in a broken home.

ONBOARDING

My cousin Elsie also got involved with a man who had a son. Elsie was good with the boy. He was with them in the summers. She packed his lunch and took him to the park.

Elsie's mother—my aunt—was not totally sure of all this at first. It was a non-traditional family and Elsie's mother was very traditional. She sewed and baked and was a teacher, even though she was brainy and probably should have been a neuroscientist; she followed convention.

It came to a head. Elsie reminded her mother that although the boy was not her biological son, he was still her stepson. Just like even though Elsie was not her mother's biological daughter, she was still her adoptive daughter. That did the trick.

This is what happens though: Everyone gets on board. At first, they are worried. They don't say this exactly, but it is clear they are not sure this is the right choice for you. But after a while you lay it out there. You say, "It may not be the way you've imagined this would go, but this is how it's going." And then there is nothing else they can do but get on board. So they ask about the kids. They start sending cards for Valentine's Day and Halloween. It's sweet.

Until it turns out it really wasn't the right choice for you. Then everyone has to untangle. The grandson disappears in the night. But no one is smirking. No one is saying, "I told you so."

CHILDLESSNESS UP

One in five American women will not give birth in their lifetime, compared to one in 10 in the 1970s. This is according to Pew. One. Two. Three. Four. Five. I count out my friends. Mid-thirties. None of us with children. Give us another 10 years and I bet we can get it down to one in four. We don't talk about it much, even those of us who do want families. What is there to say? It is like holding your hand up to your face during a scary movie and then parting your fingers. Sometimes my friend will say, "We all know our eggs are going bad," as a joke. Sometimes she'll read me something from the *New York Times* about infertility. I tell her I don't want to know. We'll cross that bridge when we come to it. At the moment, I can't even find where the bridge is on the map.

Pew goes on to explain that the most educated women—those with master's and doctorate degrees—are the most likely to never have children. Not a huge surprise. These women are busy doing other things. But when I think about it more, it makes me laugh. Read another way, Pew seems to be saying that having no children is the smart choice. One out of five female doctors recommends it.

SOMEONE ELSE'S THINGS

My cousin Elsie is telling me about her living situation when she was married—it didn't work out with her and the man with the son. She and I have bonded over the fact our lives have taken such a similar route.

She tells me about how when her husband's sister passed away they took in the woman's cat. Then, of course there was Charlie, her husband's son from his first marriage. Then they got her husband's son's cat from the first marriage, because the ex-wife decided she didn't want it anymore.

Elsie says, "We had a full house, but none of it was mine. I just wanted something that was mine, whether it was cats or boys. I just wanted something that was mine."

I know what she means. I remember daydreaming once about having a child with James. And my first thought was that it would be mine. Not ours, but mine. He already had his.

YOU ALWAYS DO THAT

"You always do that, you always try to force it." A friend is trying to make sure I don't make another mistake with my love life. She's right. There was a lot of trying to make it work.

When I sign up for an online dating site, I give her the password and tell her to do it for me and let me know when she finds Mr. Right. She does, she contacts him, and then he doesn't respond.

Convinced something must be wrong—this is the guy—she emails the company to see if there is a glitch. They send back a form letter saying, "We know it is hard not to hear back from someone, but remember he might be busy or out of town. Give him time. Meanwhile, we will send him a message saying you are VERY interested in him." This is what it has come to.

My friend is not sure why this is so hard. Why didn't Steve from Park Ridge write back? She is married, she has two kids, and as we talk on the phone she leans away to explain to the little one that these are his choices: it is this or nothing.

SWIM TEAM

When I moved to Chicago, I ended up in an apartment a few blocks from an indoor city pool. I started going a couple times a week. There were three lanes. Fast, medium and slow. In the slow lane, older gentlemen congregated in the shallow end and chatted—never swimming one stroke. I swam in the medium lane. Each breath was an isolated moment. I counted them out. One, two, three, four, until finally I could swim a full 20 minutes without stopping.

It was always crowded, at least four or five people to a lane. I smiled at my fellow swimmers but kept to myself. Then one day someone hollered at me that it was time I moved to the fast lane. He was smiling and joking. We began talking and then someone else joined in and then someone else. Afterward we all went out for a beer. We made plans to swim together the next week and the week after that. We were a motley crew: a teacher, a general contractor, a businessperson and me. We started going to movies and gathering at each other's houses for dinner. It was just what I needed.

I did end up moving to the fast lane. I decided that being the slowest one in the fast lane is better than being the fastest one in the medium lane.

POLTERGEIST

It's been years now.

I go to bed in my nice apartment in Chicago with my nice white down comforter. The evening is cool and a breeze is coming in my window. I read a book of poetry about a little red monster that fills me with joy and then turn off my light. Tomorrow I will wake up and go to work at the desk in my home office: a freelance writer. Things are in place. I have very few complaints.

Then I dream: I am at James's house with his new wife and they are having a party. Alex and Caleb are there. They are the ages they would be now, teenagers. When I arrive, they are sleeping in a dog's kennel in the front hall because there isn't room for them anywhere else. In the dream I am upset by this, but the boys don't seem to mind. Mainly, they are just disappointed in me. They ask me where I have been. Caleb takes on a scolding tone, saying I shouldn't have left them for so long. Alex is wearing red feety pajamas. I apologize.

When I am in that space that is neither here nor there, just as one wakes, I think, "It's okay. Lori will make sure they never sleep in a cage." Which is absurd, but true.

The dream stays with me all day and into the next day. My chest is filled with clay. My throat fused. It has been years, for goodness' sake.

TRUTH

What would James say if he were telling this story? There are moments in life that we remember more clearly than others, like italics on the page. They are signposts that guide us through our own history. I see the cookie dough. I see Lori in a white dress. I see the Pink Lady's Slipper. What does James see? What are the moments that my mind does not even recall, that he conjures in love and anger and disappointment?

There is no truth. Truth is like the silly putty warmed in the sun on Caleb's windowsill. It will take whatever shape you want to give it.

NOSTALGIA

An old friend is describing how depressed he was when he was in graduate school. He tells how he would get a six-pack of beer and go back to his room in student housing and drink it alone while he read Jung and Marx until three or four in the morning.

"Sometimes I miss it," he says.
"What?" I ask. "Graduate school?"
"And being depressed."
"You miss being depressed?"

I'm not sure I understand him correctly, but then he says: "I can remember the shape of the leaves outside my window. And how it felt, walking home carrying the beer. I can remember everything."

AFTERMATH

I ask my cousin Elsie about Charlie, her ex-stepson. She tells me that at first when it ended, Charlie's dad wouldn't let her see him. It's not clear why. Or maybe it is, but she doesn't go into it, because after a while he changed his mind. They could see each other. So Elsie took Charlie out for the day.

She says:

"It was Christmas and Charlie was in town visiting. So, I texted Charlie and asked if he wanted to get together the next day. We were texting back and forth and then at the end he texted me *I love you*, and I thought, was that a mistake? But then I thought no, I think he means that.

When I picked him up, there he was, a 13-year-old boy. A completely different kid. The last time we'd spent much time together he was 11. I mean, now his voice was really low and he had a little dark," she puts her finger just above her lip.

"It was awkward at first. What do you talk about? But we ended up having a good day. We went to GameStop because he had a bunch of gift certificates from Christmas and there were all these other boys there who had been cooped up for days because of the snow and they were going crazy and I was there with all the other parents. Then we went to see a movie.

I took him back and dropped him off and we were sitting in the car and I said, 'You know, if I don't see you for a long time it isn't because of you it's because of other stuff going on' and he said, 'I know, Elsie' . . . I know Elsie, was what he said."

OCTAVIA'S TRUE LOVE

When your husbands were away, for months or years at a time, who killed the spider in the den? Who told you that your thick, rope-like hair was something to admire? Who sat next to you at your dinner parties, making everyone laugh?

It was your son. The only man you could ever count on. You were surrounded by daughters, then this son. A man who could not disown you. A man whose warm, youthful skin could make you lightheaded with just one touch. Not because you wanted to possess it, but because it was already yours and you couldn't believe your luck. Everyone loved him; he was that sort of man. But you loved him most, loved him above all things.

You withstood the death of your first husband and the divorce from your second. You withstood it all with grace and propriety. But when it came to the death of your son, you were not to be consoled. Like a low-class woman you fainted in the street. Gutted. They say you mourned him until your own death.

Is this the difference in the love for a husband or a child? From one, you move on. Sometimes so easily it troubles you. From the other, you never do.

TWO AT A TIME

A woman I knew gave birth to twins, when she already had two children at home. It was a surprise. She also worked full time and was highly successful. She said that when she was pregnant she would go into meetings and women would start pouring out their infertility stories. Like a stone to be rubbed or a tea to be drunk, they thought they could capture some of her luck. She said she felt bad. She felt like she was gloating, proclaiming that she had her babies two at a time.

But then, when the babies were maybe nine months old, she and I had lunch. She was wearing a nice black dress and heels. There was grey in her hair, but that was not new. It ran in her family and made her seem faintly mysterious. At lunch, she was exasperated.

She was my editor at a company I freelanced for and they had offered her a promotion. They were growing and they wanted her to grow with them. "I think I am going to have to say no," she said, shocked herself and waiting for me to register shock. "I have infant sons at home." Again, she said this as if someone had just whispered it to her and it was the first time she was finding out.

I said something about making choices in order to be happy. I said something about how having it all seemed like more of a myth than a reality. She said, "That's not what I've been told." She was now thinking that she could have it all, but maybe not all at the same time. If there was anyone who could manage it, I knew it would be her. She was highly efficient. She had her babies two at a time.

EGGS

"We're going to put the girls on ice," is how Katie says it—she's talking about her eggs. She has no choice: she has breast cancer. Radiation then Tamoxifen for five years, which comes with a long list of warnings that starts with *Using this medication while pregnant can harm your unborn baby.* No babies for five years.

We are on the phone talking, our primary occupation for 15 years now. I know it is 15 because in every card she has ever sent me she counts it down: "Can you believe we have been friends for four years?" Seven years. 15 years. And I guess this is why, so that when life turns out differently than you expected there is someone to remind you how you got here.

"Are you nervous?" I ask. She'll have to pump her body with hormones before the procedure. She says no, I just might get a number of calls from her in various emotional states. That I already knew.

A few weeks later, I go out to see her for a visit. Katie and I both grew up in the Midwest. Now she lives in Boston. She had emailed me and said she needed me to come. She wasn't sure if she could go through her first few rounds of radiation, otherwise. My suitcase is in her guestroom. We are on her couch and getting right down to it.

She is beautiful with her blond hair, short stubby fingers and slightly greasy skin from worrying. But, you can't talk about cancer and beauty. It's cliché. Nobody can hear it. Just like it means so little when someone says *clean as a whistle* or something *cost them an arm and leg.* In French they say *it cost the eyes right out of my head.* Now that's something that resonates. Which body parts is this going to cost? We don't know yet.

We do know that she is going to harvest her eggs. Recently the procedure went from experimental to mainstream. Due to flash-freezing technology known as vitrification, it is open season on eggs. To vitrify literally means *to change or make into glass through heat.* Tiny glass human eggs like dewdrops.

When I look up egg harvesting online one of the steps in the procedure is "Identify the Eggs." After they have been extracted each individual egg is identified under a microscope then frozen. Each one is about the size of the period that ends this sentence. What are their identifying characteristics? One half of a maybe human—does it have blond hair? Does it have her eyes?

She tells me about her appointment with the fertility counselor and I want to know all about it. What will happen? How much will it cost? I want to know because I am concerned about her, but not just her.

SO MUCH TO SAY

The guy salutes the girl as he walks in the door of the coffee shop. She has long red hair, thin limbs and wide eyes like a marionette. She offers up a husky laugh and says, "I can't believe you're here again." He is tall with a goofy smile. I am across the room, but I can hear them. We all can.

The two can't talk fast enough. He is back. She is there almost every day, it seems. They find this coincidence unbelievable. He says something I can't make out and she says that oh, yes, she has seen that band. They're great. She is particularly fond of the xylophone. It haunts her. And how is the studying going? Not well, she got started too late. Didn't get to the coffee shop until two, slept until noon. Just couldn't get out of bed.

He has been thinking, he has been thinking about the idea of verisimilitude since they last talked. He has been thinking about it as it applies to his dreams. This is another coincidence because she has been thinking the same thing. She says, "It is like my waking life is the dream." He knows what she means. He knows.

He says he is on his way somewhere and just stopped in for iced tea. When he gets his tea, he goes right back to her. Already they seem to be tethered. They can't stop talking. There is so much to say. There is so much to say. There is so much to say.

It is 4:30pm on a Thursday in September and the heat has finally broken. The woman at the counter talks to everyone as they come in. People feel like being friendly. But not me. I want to smack that girl. How dare she take up all the words and leave me with nothing to say? With nothing I even want to say. Can it really be that just because of those doll-eyes all those platitudes seem new?

I am here to do work. In the marketing report I am finishing I find that women aged 35 to 54 are highly likely to look for products that help fight aging. Women over age 55 aren't as interested. Surprising. But maybe not—maybe they have become resigned to their situation. The younger group hasn't accepted it yet. They want to keep fighting. They want to smack that girl.

TUPPERWARE

I look through the Tupperware and select the container depending on how likely it is I think I will see the man again. The flimsiest ones, the ones the commercials assure you you won't mind losing, I have to keep replenishing. Over dinner at my house—usually the fourth date—these men say things that convince me this can't move forward.

Like the guy who had a brilliant solution to the abortion debate: just create a technology that can move an unwanted fetus into the body of a woman who can't have children. He said because his ideas were out of the box, people usually didn't react to them well at first. I pointed out that his plan left out the emotional side of the equation. He took home a small serving of penne arrabiata.

There was the guy who explained how all of his friends were getting divorces. Even the ones who had once seemed the perfect couples, so in love. We talked about how rough relationships were and then sized each other up across the table. We had chicken tortilla soup. I considered not sending leftovers home with him at all.

I imagine my Tupperware crowding their cupboards, or left in the communal fridges at their workplaces. A strange lid, a strange size, doesn't fit with anything else they've got. Who knows where it came from?

The best pieces, the ones with hard rubber lids that my mother got for me in a set one Christmas, I never send home with anyone. They remain neatly stacked in my cupboard. So far, no one has been worth the risk.

TALKING TO A FRIEND WHO DATED A MAN WITH KIDS

"It is strange because you're nothing. You're something. You *are* something. But really you are nothing."

THE MOST PAINFUL MOMENT

The most painful moment is later.

Caleb and Alex came into my life too early. I wasn't ready. Then I had to be. And then, like the last pink moment of the setting sun, they were gone. Right then—in absence—my own biological clock started ticking.

A dark spot burned into my retina, I keep trying to blink and see something different.

SOLIDARITY

Riding home on the El. It is the middle of December, nearing the shortest day of the year. I am coming home from meetings downtown and already the sun hovers just above the buildings. The train isn't crowded this time of day. I stare out the window and daydream.

There is a woman sitting across the aisle who I do not notice for a long time. She is a little older than me, or at least she appears to be. She is wearing tennis shoes. What is significant is that she is crying. Not just crying, weeping. Silently.

I glance around the train to see if anyone else is looking. No one seems to be paying attention.

What should I do? What do you do? I worry that if I do anything I will regret it. Is she crazy? Imbalanced. Or maybe if I say something she will just talk to me, for too long, on and on.

"Are you okay?" I ask.

She looks at me for a moment, then tells me she is fine. I can see she is a little embarrassed that I have caught her doing something we normally hide behind bathroom doors.

"Are you sure?"

She is sure.

"Is there anything I can do?"

She tells me no. She is fine. Everything is fine. I nod.

Then I do something that surprises us both. I reach my hand across the aisle and take hold of her hand. She looks at me again, unsure. I smile softly and she squeezes my hand. She is still weeping. I notice that her gloves are cheap, but then so are mine.

"Things are hard sometimes," I say to both of us. Neither one of us speaks after that. Every few minutes she squeezes.

We hold hands the rest of the trip—10 stops in all.

OCTAVIA'S HONOR

Her likeness was engraved on coins. She couldn't have done much better. Isn't that what we all hope for when we have played the martyr? Someday everyone will understand our value. Someday they will all be sorry.

NO RELATION

James got remarried. The woman he married has a daughter. One of the last times we talked, he said that he was beginning to understand how I might have felt. He was beginning to understand what it was like to spend so much time with a child that wasn't your own. He said he liked the girl, liked her fine, but it wasn't like he couldn't wait to see her. He admitted, with some trepidation, that it was hard. Very hard. He said he didn't feel that he was all that good at it.

I told him that over time, years and years, the relationship would change. It would.

SINGLE

Katie says to me, "I remember when I first started working. I was 25. Some of the women I worked with were in their mid-thirties and they weren't married. I remember thinking *what are they doing?* I wasn't going to do that." Katie works in international public health. She regularly travels to places like Ghana and Tanzania, as do her co-workers.

Katie and I are on the phone, again. We are planning her birthday—this time she is going to come and visit me. Everything is going smoothly with her treatment. Her arm did swell up a little once because of the lymph node they took out. But otherwise, smooth. She sent me a book called *Anti-Cancer* and included a photocopied recipe for roasted cauliflower. Right now she is reading, *It's Not You: 27 (Wrong) Reasons You're Single*.

I remember that, too. At my first job, there was a woman who was maybe 37 and she met this guy on the bus and they ended up getting married and everyone was so excited for her. But I remember wondering what was up, that it took her that long. It seemed to point to some flaw.

I never wondered what had come before—all the things in those 37 years that might have happened.

PRINCE CHARMING

My niece is coloring a picture of Barbie dressed like Cinderella dancing with Prince Charming. We are downstairs in her playroom. I am making shapes out of play dough. Every once in a while she looks over and tells me she likes what I am making, which at that moment is a very long snake wrapped into a spiral. She is in a good mood. At other times she might not be so encouraging.

Later that afternoon she is going to a birthday party for Brandon: a boy who lives up the street and is in her class. He is turning seven and she is the only girl invited to the party. She has taken this as a serious compliment. She tells me that she likes Brandon and she knows he likes her too. She says they sit together at lunch. Then she says, "I can't stop thinking about him. I mean, I just can't stop."

There are only a handful of people on this earth who make me so happy I can't help but smile when I am with them and my niece and her siblings are at the top of that list. I smile at her now. I ask her what it is she is thinking about Brandon and she shakes the hair from her face and says, "Oh, I don't know," a little exasperated. She returns to the dress she is filling in with pink crayon. Later, she will thoughtfully choose her own party outfit.

Already, I think. Already it begins.

YOUNG LOVE

Riding home on the El. They can't be more than fifteen. A boy and a girl. The girl is wearing white nail polish and the boy is wearing black-rimmed glasses. It is the first day of spring. Not the first official day of spring, but the first day when the temperature is warmer than expected and light will dally in the sky later than expected. People unzip their coats. Come bedtime, the alleys will be full of talk and shouts.

The train is crowded and so they share a single seat. She sits on his lap. This is just the way they want it. His hand on her ass is familiar, protective. He is smaller than her, thin, while she has developed. She takes off his glasses and brushes his black hair to the side. He blinks. They are talking all this while. About what, I don't know. He adjusts his hand and circles it around her waist. She doesn't seem to notice. Their bodies are not their own.

At some point, the boy catches me watching. I try to smile, but he stares me down, his face tough. Why so defiant? What does he think I'm thinking? What does he think I'll do? Even my gaze is intruding on his territory.

At Irving Park they get off together. They hold hands. He laughs at something she says and his face is so soft, so sweet and young. She does that to him. For him.

FACEBOOK FRIENDS

Sometimes I look up Alex and Caleb on Facebook. I'm not their "friend," so I can only see their profile pictures and a few things about them. Caleb has "liked" some sports teams and celebrities, things like the Cincinnati Bengals and some rapper I don't know. Neither of these seem too far off from the boy I knew, so that is a comfort. He has a bunch of friends and their little faces belie children trying not to be—especially the girls.

It is so much like stalking an ex-boyfriend that it makes me uncomfortable. I don't do it often. But every once in a while, I just have to remind myself that they are real. I want to see that they are growing up, that they are doing things, that despite the void in my understanding there is something to know.

This need has lessened with time. Probably because I have accepted the way things have turned out. Or maybe, it is really because my imagination is having a hard time keeping up. They are starting to be too far gone.

MARSHMALLOWS

Aadit knows just the place. A small restaurant with Christmas lights still hung—even though it is January—tucked away among the tall buildings in downtown Chicago. Korean BBQ. The two words I find hard to fit together. But I don't say this to Aadit, whose family is from India, who grew up in New York and wears brown leather shoes that come to a point at the toe. Who opens every door for me. Whose name I have just learned I have been mispronouncing for the last month.

Our fire pit is right in the middle of the table. We order Kobe beef and duck. Shiitake mushrooms. But for dessert, I insist on the s'mores—there is a picture on the menu. A few squares of Hershey's chocolate, store brand graham crackers, and two large marshmallows on a plate. The simple beauty of it makes me happy.

But what I'm really thinking about is the time James and I took the boys camping in Kentucky in October and each camper had lugged along elaborate Halloween decorations to spruce up their site. How the boys went off to explore and how moments later James panicked, imagining them kidnapped or falling down a well. He went in search of them, while I got out hot dogs and the makings of s'mores. Then I sat waiting for the boys to be found and him to return, which was usually the way things were then.

They hadn't gone far and soon they all returned together. Alex ate the marshmallows right out of the bag, while James tried to show Caleb how to rotate his over the fire and I tried not to move, taking in the stillness in the woods around us, not wanting to disrupt the stillness that had finally descended on his heart.

That is what I'm thinking of, roasting marshmallows with a handsome man who carefully helps me remove the hot sugar from the spit and whose apartment, high above the city, I will go to later. There will be a kind of stillness there, too.

IN TOWN FOR OTHER REASONS

In town for other reasons, I drive past the old house. There are trucks in the drive and a spattering of toys on the lawn. A teenage girl swings on a new swing set. I pull my car over to the side of the road and try to imagine each of the rooms within. Have they left the paint the same? The yellow kitchen, the living room a rusty brown? From what I can see, they don't seem to care much for decorating.

I glance down the street to get my bearings, and when I look back I have a memory of James standing in the doorframe, his hair falling over one eye, the boys flying out from behind him, coming to greet me or to run around the lawn or both, saying my name with urgency as if they have something they must tell me—which is simply that I am here and they are here. I can see them so clearly. Their silhouettes dance around the lawn, past the girl on the swing.

Perhaps they are tucked away inside and all I must do is ask to see them. Perhaps they will come out and we will play kickball as dusk settles in and James will have to remind me not to try so hard to win—they are only little kids after all.

But of course, that is silly. They are not little kids. Bodies different, faces changed, the children I see dancing on the lawn no longer exist. But for me—perhaps like me—they are stuck here. Singing, sprinting, calling my name, their echo forever marking the day's descent into night: the golden hour.

ACKNOWLEDGMENTS

Grateful acknowledgment is made to the editors and readers of the following journals and magazines where some of these pieces originally appeared in various forms: *Prairie Schooner, Salon, The New South, Exit 7,* and *MAYDAY.*

Thank you to my mentors and friends Samrat Upadhyay and Scott Russell Sanders, who taught me so much about literature and life. To Alyce Miller for introducing me to the flash form. Roberta Kwok for being my coach and constant encourager. True friends Chris Harvey, Tracy Truels, Megan Savage, and Amelia Martens. Alessandra Simmons for bringing my writing life full circle.

For allowing me to call upon our conversations and friendships in this book: Sara Beanblossom, Erin Hasselberg, Nichole Lowery, and Danna Folkers. To Jill Nielsen-Farrell for her grace. Sophia, Roman, and Mila, you are my joy.

Special thanks to Diane Goettel and Black Lawrence Press. Justin Santora for his powerful representations of the Midwest. Megan Stielstra for the way she is in the world. Amy Danzer. Ragdale and Regin Igloria. Indiana University's M.F.A. program.

My deepest love and gratitude to Dona and Phil Carter, always. And finally, to the Nilan boys, who changed my life.

Photo: Lisa Anderson

Paula Carter's essays have appeared in *The Southern Review*, *Kenyon Review, Salon, TriQuarterly* and *Prairie Schooner*. Based in Chicago, she is a part of the live-lit community and is a company member with 2nd Story. She holds an M.F.A. from Indiana University, Bloomington, where she was the fiction editor for the *Indiana Review*. She has taught writing at Indiana University, the University of Kentucky, and Concordia University Chicago.